A Guide To Stop Fear And Prevent Problems At The RNC.
Find What You Need From A To Z Within This Guide.

(The New Peaceful City of Love)

Who says our City, Cleveland, Ohio, cannot have as much peace in it as the City of brotherly love?

For the protestors and demonstrators:
this could help keep everyone safe!

This is a Spiritual Way of Guidance Led by Common Sense!

Dedication

Dedicated to bringing back some of the good days to the lives of the people in and around Cleveland. One of the biggest tasks is to rehab the longest pedestrian foot bridge in Cleveland, Ohio. I walked across it many times as a child. It was 680 feet long and connected East 65th and Sidaway (Polish American) with Kinsman Avenue (African American), between East 69th and East 70th Street. The bridge burned during racial tension in 1966 and still stands abandoned. I think it would be wonderful to restore the bridge to its original beauty, and the peace that can go along with it.

There is a need to revitalize this bridge along the revitalization of the only waterfall in Cleveland. Both could be wonderful tourist attractions.

Foreword

Having a new revelation of the word of God is like seeing a new nova that is first seen by way of a telescope from a distance that only a few can see because it seems so far away and the darkness that it had to come out of was a blinding force that could not be seen into at first. Oh well, this is only a picture of what I see in my heart and now it is on paper for others to see. I thank the Lord for it must be his will.

I am calling out around the world to get ready to learn a new revelation. It was hard to do but the unseen poison that needs to be revealed is shown to sow the seeds to good health.

Welcome to someone who can now stay out of and not go into, or get out of bondage as a slave for the devil's principles of actions that can be free with the help in one or more of the books mentioned.

Everyone has to pay homage or dues to the Lord and by just taking your time to learn this, it is what you are doing in one perspective and it alone allows you to move on to the next step where he wants to take you if you are willing to follow him.

Introduction

Hello to All

We at Bound to heaven Publishing are putting certain measures in place to help prevent a possible calamity at the RNC in Cleveland, Ohio. We suggest also that you utilize the tools that are available through Bound to Heaven Publishing/Ministries. They consist of a number of books that will make others able to adjust themselves and the atmosphere around them, to create a more heavenly state of peacefulness in order to avoid trouble. There is a book to help stop the protesting that goes the wrong way that creates riots or violence.

Question: if you had a pound of prevention that would create a miracle, what would you do with it? Is this the preventive measure from the Lord that prayers brought forth? Do not figure. Come see or just get it to know it for yourself.

An understanding of how to be a part of snatching the veil of darkness off that is hovering over Cleveland that he people and government has put in place is what we must do. I am talking about the upcoming RNC that has already reared up its face in other places that protestors act a fool in.

Now if the government gives a $50 million ticket to prevent and protect and if need be fight off, the ungodly foe that may come to steal, kill and destroy, we know that it is not an all the way good thing.

Therefore, we have to put a plan into action and if we look at the DNC and think of what may be going on there do we want to or need to at least try to make our City better or do we stand by and let whatever happens, happen? I think not, I know not. If we want to consider our city equal to the best of cities in America, then we fight to make it known. If we in Cleveland have made a way to move up in life then we go for it. There is no time to sit around with our morals stuck on stupid.

Now even the people that are going to vote for Trump should take part in this process of stopping the violence to let the country and world know that it is not what we are about no matter whose side we are on and if the process starts off like that in a violent way, it may continue. Therefore, whatever side you are on, be civil and don't commit yourself to violence and let's make the City of Cleveland as if it is the twin to Philadelphia, a city of brotherly love also.

We can treat this as a real celebration beforehand and not like we are at war because we have learned how to also end the spiritual ones that wanted to become a part of the RNC to make trouble as an undercover spice that has been caught and dismissed from the presence of the land and the people.

People, People, People

Are we going to sit around and act like we are sitting ducks because of a man who has so many strings tied to him that can make things not so good. He brings along trouble with his presence. What I mean is what can be done about it? First, the misguided energy at the RNC because of a candidate, then if we have an anecdote to stop a problem of people that may be at a protest that can turn into a riot that can get out of control, are we going to do or try to do something to prevent it? I would like to think so and here is what we can do.

Let's become cop-blockers and do something so we don't need them to stop anything. Here is a plan that the Lord has approved. Foremost, it is a learning process and it needs to be on a layman level. Therefore it can be as if it is a phenomenon presence of work on paper. Now it is up to the people to know the truth that can be in their hand to use and do what is right with.

Find the ounce of faith that makes a pound of cure and that is worth a miracle that fixes prevention. The stopping of a crisis may require an ounce of love that comes from the Lord. The love can come in many ways but he is where the people should go to for help.

If we at Bound to Heaven Publishing/Ministries make sure there is nothing missing in the information that has been put together that means nothing can be broken. Now is the time for all people to join in to help make sure this is a successful endeavor with endless results, wherever you live become a part of the new town of Cleveland and the continued growth of its renovation.

This is a complete comprehensive plan and will cater to any other event with all details needed included.

Now could all of this be a part of the new parallel universe to come? Now we have to divide and conquer all of what could be developed as a bad situation. To stop this from happening, the following books are recommended so you can find the information you need to do the job that needs to be done.

This is somewhat of an introduction to a new book also titled, _What's Going On?_, (A Way to Create Hope in the People and Country so all Can Prosper, with Cleveland, Ohio being first on the list at this time in history).

What's Going On?

The book brings landmarks back to the forefront of the people of Cleveland, such as the Sidaway Bridge and the only waterfall in Cleveland, Ohio. It takes the dark side of the Kingsbury Run murders and places hope on one day stopping this kind of madness. The book is a challenging read that develops insight to make this a better world by a local historian that has first-hand experience and knowledge about this.

This book was written to create a firestorm of thinking before the peace movement takes place. The need to stop the kind of negative reactions that Donald Trump has been causing around the country can be doused out before it hits

Cleveland. The knowledge in the book will help to burn it out and at the same time set a fire in the body of Christians that has a way in which it works to stop a fire by starting one that kills them both. This is done in real life in some cases.

The information in this book and others that have been authored by Bro. Bush, has added something that may be better than the free RNC service guide. It teaches you how to protect yourself at protests, and all other venues that have anything to do with the RNC. I do suggest people get the service guide by the RNC Committee. You can go online to Cleveland.com to get the information about it.

Added Blessings are Within This Book and All Others:

A Promise to Help Prevent Violence at Protests and Rallies in America

We can put a wrench in the plans Satan has to rain down on the RNC with some kind of hellish act. The party pooper's plan has gone to crap, thanks to the revealing of what is really going on. Now before anyone goes to a protest, they should get a copy.

The book has many things in mind to teach the political arena. First is to learn to get along in order to complete what may be on the agenda without all the backbiting. Second, to stop the upcoming process of what could become a riot or hands on fight between people who are out of touch with reality by way of a satanic presence that can and will make trouble from the chaos and confusion along with the disagreements that start up a kind of spiritual warfare that come down to earth.

Now if you can put aside what you believe or don't want to believe and don't think about this and let it be known as an imponderable/ponderable process people need to know that it expands in a state of reality and can affect people on earth.

At Bound to Heaven Publishing/Ministries, we are making things ready to have a good experience at the RNC for all involved and others in the surroundings community we are crossing all "t's" and dotting all "i's".

Ending Political Wars in America

This book will help create a healthy environment. It contains three main points to enhance the political arena: one is to learn to get along in order to complete what may be on the agenda without all of the backbiting; two is to stop the upcoming process of what could be rioting or hands-on fighting among people who are out of touch with reality by way of a satanic presence that can and will make trouble from the chaos and confusion, along with any disagreements that start up a kind of spiritual warfare that lands on earth through people; and three, it helps us to not get caught off-guard by way of any potential threat to harm people that may occur due to people being distracted because of our own issues. We can work with local authorities as well as homeland security, if need be, using our eyes and ears.

You can put aside what you believe, or don't want to believe, and not think about this and let it become known as imponderable/ponderable. Either way, people need to know that it exists in a state of reality that can adversely affect them.

At this time, we are targeting the two political conventions, RNC, DNC because of the fear that they may take a turn for the worse. This can be stopped with the assistance of the knowledge within the book.

The Devil Passed Me By

This book provides the complete blueprint of how this is done. Warning, without the instructions, if we as a people go into a fight about whatever decision we think is right or wrong about this event it will not matter, because we are setting ourselves up for a big loss.

We can prevent a spiritual warfare from landing on earth. There comes a time when we do not have only commercial tools to fix something when it is broken to stop it from getting even worse like a dam breaking loose.

If an unwise person predicts a major problem is going to happen in the city of Cleveland, we as godly people can stop the process, with the truth about the counterfeit way it came about in the first place, before the nominated candidate said there will be a riot if he is not nominated. Now at a time when there is apprehension and tension, it seems quite devilish to make comments like that.

Who is it that predicted it? A troubled man. What does this man have that got him where he is at? Being somewhat business savvy with a degree of success. Saying all this I feel this person has a personal problem; it is called towerism. Is this new? No. Can it be fixed? Yes but not in time, with this person personally, before the voting process stops. Therefore, we have to fix the atmosphere, by removing the wick from the wicked that some people have in them to show them how to not go to the powder keg.

The RNC status has put some panic in the lives of people in Cleveland, Ohio. To make this go away, we have been invited to a live performance that we can be in. The theme of the play that unfolds in the book is real life to show how the devil can pass by Cleveland, Ohio with all the harm that he wants to do. Let's make some good history come to life in the time that we live in.

Ending Spiritual Warfare in America

The real level of rights that people have been denied is one thing. It is spiritual rights to the gifts. The lack of them has caused the division of people throughout the world. It is the real thief of all times that has turned more people against themselves then all of the wars of nations that were against each other, than all of them put together and the in-house fighting between one ethnicity of people against another. That is what the lack of spiritual rights that has been misplaced or missing in the presence of the lives of people has done.

Therefore, we reclaim the right to have spiritual rights delivered once again to the land and the people who will appreciate it on all levels of showing it as we live among one another no matter what color.

There have been missions that have been put together for the blessings of the people for their hearts to see the light of God, in order to not let Satan tie anyone in the warfare with Satan to lose a fight that only the Lord can win. Now you can learn the rules: how to stay out of the way.

Fixing What is Broken in America by Stopping Towerism

The tricks are in the process that Satan takes some people who take him for granted - the ones who think they know enough about him to play inside of his fire. They may be the one who he sets up on a pedestal to make them feel good about what they do. More so he puts all the love they need in their life in a way that blinds them because they would have gotten it anyway. It makes the person think they have to have it all to keep them who may be there so they pay the cost to the demon way of living to keep them in a presence of wealth. They get so high off of this kind of life they would rather die than give it up.

They get the same treatment that Eve got an apple that makes them feel their life is so set it blinds them more to a level of non-reality existence they can see and subconsciously they feel as they are a demi-god. Once there it is the place that comes along with the title of being a towerist.

Then without the true perspective of what is going on in one's self and the heart repenting before the mind does it, they get stuck and it becomes a lost pathway that gets harder and harder to come out of, unless you get a blessing of a special kind and the only one I know of comes from the freedom that the word of God can supply to give the light out of this kind of darkness.

The Recovery of the U.S. Government, The Power of Knowing "No" (the Beginning)

As people in the United States, we are in need of standing in correction of ourselves and if we do not look at where we are wrong in the things we are doing, we may be thinking too highly of ourselves as having some kind of control that can get someone in hot water or burnt before they know it.

To the world and the people in it, we need not fear the radical factions out there. As I will say more than once, we need to fear the wrath of Father Time alongside Mother Nature that can unleash a force of darkness that will harm the nation and cripple the people all by its self.

We are already witnessing the droughts, floods and fires. Therefore, now is the best time to get our houses in order before it becomes a part of all of our doorsteps in ways that are unmentionable. This is a great time to retool our country, but we have to stop being afraid of learning what it takes, no matter who it came from as long as they are giving the right principles that are in line with the Lord.

The Disconnection of Extremism

What causes some people to want to become a terrorist? The dysfunction (they feel) in the country and government and in them creates unhappiness overall. They feel like a misfit in the USA because of this they go against it. There is more to this process; this is a brief understanding or a tip of the iceberg.

That is what the prince of darkness likes to come in to make them think they see some light into the darkness that blinds them to the truth. When this happens, they may not win the personal war that some people face as I went through in my life at one time but thank God I saw the real light. Now it is a wish that all see the light and is able to show others what it is and means that leads the way to eternal life.

This is a part of the fishing for those who are lost in the sea of darkness, who cannot see, in life. What happen is no self-guidance to understand they are living in the promised-land I call America? This can be fixed so they will not be an element of surprise by the enemy within themselves that has to be defeated with love for one's self. There is a two-edged sword that goes with this that you will find out about.

A Peace Offering for the People and the Police

This book has a forerunner to it that is included within the book. The material was released during the time of the problems the City of Cleveland, Ohio had at a time when protesters were at odds with the police. There is a fact that preventive help and this is the goal that all of the information provides. It is to show both sides a better way to get along also that we have problems that are bigger than ourselves and we can put our heads together and fix the problem. This book has been promoted throughout the country, at the same time when lots of civil unrest was going on. Did it help to stabilize the country?

With its resources there is no way to say it did not but its faith and hope in what we are doing for the good of humanity. At Bound to Heaven Publishing/Ministries, we would like to believe so.

Notification

There is more than one way for a spiritual war to come about and cause harm. We have focused on about four major ways it can enter into the environment of people by way of different confusion. The books, having individual methods for therapy, provide pathways to end going into going into the dilemma of this kind of confusion and chaos.

All of the books have a satisfying platform that it relates upon but it can tie into unification of a process of learning. We as people need to have the understanding of not having any kind of competition about this and the reason why is there is an endless level of thoughts and principles that do not need to go on and on without a conclusion to it. This can be a cut and dry state of moving forward that has no religious presence within to put a ceiling on learning. This is why it is based on a spiritual growth plan.

All of the above mentioned books (and more) can be found at Createspace.com (in paperback format) and/or Amazon.com (in eBook format). Search Bro. Tracy Book for purchase information.

To all the people if we are going to embrace the future and place truth in it, we need to not continually cut the spiritual activity out of the modern day adventures of our lives. It must be also embraced as a new format that shows it can also supply a need that doesn't require greed or malice or injustice that has any kind of towerism within its principles.

The Lord Has Made a Crossing

Is this something that has the same presence like the crossing at the red sea if the people did not cross or stopped in the middle of it they would parish!

Don't fear crossing this bridge.
It has been built with and up from love!

Who really has the fear of receiving wisdom?
Anyone who has the fear of using it only!

We can use this power of love to do this with spiritual skills

People now have an opportunity in America to correct themselves and the country. With the help of this information, people can be a part of helping to open the flood gates of Heaven so manna can rain down! At the least or best it is a blessing!

Now we are at a cross-road? Are we in Cleveland going to continue building up or let someone come into our City and develop an attitude to tear it down? The people will be here for a 14-day period and they can if we let them take a year or more out of our progress. Are we that naïve? Hell no, that will not prevail in Cleveland, Ohio, a downfall of harm in any shape or form.

The shoreline needs to be informed of the visual that is taken place from A to Z also the inland areas to keep us safe from the wrong kind of foreign intruders.

One pound of prevention can create a miracle every time.

For the Body of Christ

To the church: We all need to go on watch. The Lord says let his people go who may be trapped under the rules of your governing them as if they have no gift of their own to be manifested through them for the Lord.

Do not fear the fire if you know the water; the fire that the Lord has in you. If you do, there is a book, *Do Not Fear the Water*. It can quench the fear to step to the plate and become a home run hitter for the Lord.

To all my sisters and brothers in Christ: can we see that this is a better than good fight that uses love. It has been approved by the Lord?

Can you help by adding your prayers that will help us to produce a greater concept that can work for all people. I feel this is just need another level of help that comes with your prayers. Thank you for any or all the help you can give. This needs to be known by everyone: make sure you include this information in your conversations.

The information is like an extra guarantee to help people see through the light to know if it is right.

Please help get this word out!

To Grow into the Right Light

To know the right opposite of a dark side of the mind side can attract you to it in a safe way through a vision that lets you know who they are as some who don't have good intentions. This means an inner sense of the wrong person that may be revealed to you in a dream can be taken to another level and can be revealed to the authorities to stop their madness. This is a part of what spiritual skills can do.

This is a place that works for the good of mankind with a two-edged sword that can cut Satan's crap if it comes at someone in two different ways at the same time. This worked for me because I had a dream that revealed two people who were raping and murdering women in my neighborhood. I helped get them caught and they went to prison.

To know more about spiritual skills look for the upcoming book that shows the understanding of how someone may become blessed with them. The book is titled, *All Peoples Handbook*.

Endorsements are many from lots of clergy and one that is known by almost all Clevelanders, Dr. Otis Moss, who has encouraged him for years to keep up his writing. There is a healing power in some things that are written and the power to protect one's self and others.

It is a tool that Tracy has used throughout over 40 years of writing that he enjoys sharing and at one time had a free spiritual reading center open to let the community come in to read the many books. He has authored about 40 books. This is his dream to reopen once again another place that all can come to experience the writing he has done.

All of the books that I have given insight on has their own way of helping to improve our nation and without your help to buy, read, and promote them it will help make us a greater place as we keep going in the future.

Within the book that mentioned previously, _What's Going On?_ there are two mistakes one the street number that was stated to be East 72nd Street and Kinsman. The number two thing is it will not take 100 years but about 10 to recover if they as Republican gets their nominee in office. This is a small process of learning with a big step of growth more can be found in conjunction with this Guide to Help Keep Cleveland Safe. The extended facts for learning more can be found within this book.

Does this help in any way that I have been approved and put on the vendors list for the upcoming RNC? It may help things remain civil. Now I would like to know once you have read a book I am informing you about, if there is any of the books I authored that should go on God's Best Seller List, email me, thank you.

We as a people have to put the issues that people have in their lives first in a way like no other time in history. We have more people being locked up in the USA than any other country in the world. We have one of the highest suicide rates that can be stopped with the right education. We have one of the largest drug problems in the world.

Saying all of this I have been blessed to know firsthand about it because I have had a problem with almost everything I write about. Here are some of the other books I have to share with others: _The Shattered Stem_, a guide to curing crack cocaine, heroin and other substance abuse; _Save Yourself From Suicide_, for those with suicidal tendencies; _Time to Stop the Abuse_, to a child or spouse, whether verbal, physical or mental; _Why Do Black Men Harm Each Other More Than Others?_, to help stop one of the biggest problems of black on black crime, that will help stop all levels of crime; _Freedom From Satan's Zone_, that can save someone a possible jail or hell sentence. There are many more books I would hope you will go to the website to review them all and get what you may need.

The plan will always be that the facts come from the word of God. The pen only makes it clear to follow. The nations of people have been kept in line to succeed or to fail by the pen that can carry more weight to it than the world may or may not ever know. Please know the freedom that comes along with the pen and its partner, paper, in God's name.

The great part of life consists of the ever changing complexion on the exterior of our lives. Now this is more important to be done on the interior of self than the exterior of the surroundings we live with or in.

The pleasant part of it is when the change takes place subtly so there is a breath of freshness that can fancy up the spirit of mankind. It is the goal of Bound to Heaven Publishing/Ministries to keep on track starting with this planning in the City of Cleveland to give people what they need to live a better life and not just put a place of outward fanciness that shows the material world.

It is the inner spirit that needs the kind of nourishment that people share and not just the brick and mortar. It is the flesh and blood process of growth that we the people must be more so committed to in life. I hope your eyes are on the real prize in life and not just the tangible ones. It is then to pursue to serve you with a love that outweighs any dollar amount that anyone has to offer they don't have blessings attached to them.

What created all of this? It is one thing that generated it. The creative power of the Lord in action within his creation that we are to be held accountable for as a tool in the way he wants to use you. If you don't know, read the book titled, _What Two Can Easily Do_. It could be a big help. It too is available on the website.

To Turn the Page

The distortion of the political presence of the RNC has taken place as I thought it might. I wrote about it in _What's Going On?_ It is about the Donald being nominated that came out in print before it happened. Furthermore, to add to that, in this book's presence of thought it would not surprise me (or others I think) that he puts a what would have been an adversary in the place of his running mate using the age old tactic, keep your enemies close to you as I think is a part of his kind of strategy of throw people off track.

Now for political reasons of stepping on to a new and higher growth, it is a fake the funk and it too should not be a shocking thing to see it done. To look for a minority, African American woman for example, is not beyond his process of developing a way, by any means necessary, to win the way he intends, no matter what!

There could be a friendly competition between the cities where both conventions will be held. There would be a small wager in which the city with the least amount of disruption during the conventions would win. Cleveland could wager one of its famous corned beef sandwiches against Philadelphia's famous cheesesteaks. The wager can be made between mayors or ministers from each city.

Bro. Bush, will take the bet because it is a peace offering to show how much love we have for our city and faith in the people to keep the peace. There comes a time when great chiefs have to meet to plan the strategies to prevent war. The prevention of a spiritual war is what we can do to end it before it begins.

To Clear Things Up

What Are the Differences Between the Two Cities?

Now do Clevelanders feel the same as the people in Philadelphia does about the convention coming to the city? No, not at this time, they have not really as much fear also the percentage of people are not shying away from the city. Do they have a chance to get more bang for their buck to go around? Yes they do.

Should or does this matter to our city planning commission? I don't know and maybe they don't either. Therefore we work with the hand we have to improve it any way we can, even though it would be a nice thing to have as many people and local politicians out and about at the same time the visitors are here and how many of them are not going to be around when company comes to town.

Excerpts from *All Peoples Handbook*

Within the writing released by Bound to Heaven Publishing/Ministries, there is a shifting which disables the negative energy that Satan produces through people. We are re-focusing our time and energy on another way to produce better results for the opening up of a new frontier, or way of life that we are adding to our lifestyle.

An Awakening

It is time to wake up if you are not happy about what is going on in and around your life. It is a time to stop making things worse than what they are or need to be. You cannot fix anything as long as you keep breaking stuff just to release frustration and pain. We are not meant to live like that. It is a trick of Satan's and it is time we stop being his tricks! Bad times come and go but we do not have to make ourselves feel good when we weigh into the bad times with our foolishness and the part of the idiosyncrasies that people have in them.

We are people who forsake each other because of this and it is a sin of ungodliness that brings destruction to the forefront and it is time to put it on the back burner and cut it off. Thank you my people.

It is Time to Destress Your Growth

To understand the workings of this process, the strategies of the therapy create thoughts or individual visions that are developed in our intangible space of a process of actions. We develop and we deliver the time plus energy to create the forecast of the weather that we can predict and permit in our lives. We are the storm chasers and creators. We are

20

also the guiding star to the heavenly parts of growth that exist within our hearts if we will it to be. Then free it to all people that we know and see. This is the wisdom of a greater part of the Lord's therapy that has been planted in you at birth. So use it, do not lose it to the tricks of Satan.

We can and must first learn how to present ourselves and others to a greater level, by using the strategies that develop the right foresight for everyone to think as a leader with positive aims and goals that keeps them as an individual but foremost as a team player that can make them capable of showing an outward state of love for self and all other people.

This can only be done if someone knows who they are and that is one of mankind's biggest problems. If we all know who we are, could we function as we should? Well, I am in awe about this question. What I will say is if we can share a respect for the people trying to find out who they are as they make their journey to the new horizon, we may have less resistance on more than one level.

Therefore, how can this become a universal process of growing a gathering of mixed souls up on one trendy process of thinking alike? I can say it sounds marginally unobtainable.

As a human but with a greater look inside of one's self, there are still endless possibilities. Therefore, the answer is to teach everyone to take a deeper and greater quest within the intention to come out with the best results that are humanly possible. Then we all may become more as one and not so divided as Satan wants but as we should have been in the first place. Then we can keep ourselves in first place all of the time because without knowing this we are not as good to and for each other.

Now if there is anyone who can stand up to themselves and walk away from themselves because of your dissatisfaction with whatever is going on that you feel may lead you to a pathway that you do not need to be a part of, bully for you. This means that you have put your faith into action. This is a human's most desired tool in life that the Lord wants you to use. It has endless possibilities that will bring the day's work to an end properly.

If there were more people who put their faith in the one fact that the Lord loves them, the world could change overnight. It might not be perfect but the change will do a world of good to a multitude of people.

What kind of road would that put us on? A road like no other that would give us the kind of fulfillment to help us know how much we need to care for others in the way that the Lord sees fit for us to and not because we may have a job that pays us to do it or because we are filled with guilt. There are some who have not learned to love for the sake of love and not because it is a reward tied up into it.

Therefore, I will try to make it known I did this in regards to not just being alive but for love also. If you get bored, friend not all can do what I do and that is keep developing a winter wonderland. What is that? That is a place that has a dream of the beauty of life on earth.

I do this because there may be one thing I cannot say, it has been said something about in the word of the Lord. I will miss about the earth as I know it now and that is the beauty of winter. It takes me back to one of my poems I wrote:

Weather the <u>Weather</u>!

Whether the <u>weather</u> be hot,
Whether the <u>weather</u> be cold,
Weather the <u>weather</u>
Whatever the <u>weather</u>
Whether you like it or not!

Good News

There is a way to help remove all fear from the people and atmosphere with a guide to prevent fear and stop problems at the RNC. Find what you need from A to Z within this guide.

People can learn what they need to know to stop having fear. The fear of this will result in a percentage of people keeping their distance from the city resulting in a loss of income. Do we need that now? Can we do something about it and if we can will we?

This is what we can do. Show the people what they need to get rid of the fear that comes in the books to help stop the crook, Satan from causing problems. What problem causes fear that causes no shows that is a loss of income also to private businesses and it decreases the city's income. Like it or not, it is the truth.

Now help me to help you to help others. When? Now!

Do we need to take another look at how we can grade ourselves as people who care about the city? Do we need to take a loss of any kind? If so, do we need to not look at a dollar loss and focus on the process of keeping people safe first? If so, it is a good combination because one does not work without the other. If you work with one, you get both. If you work with none, then none is what you get. It could be the eye opener of the century that can keep on working for the good of humanity for always.

Who is paying attention or hearing me? Can we not only fix some of the things that are wrong together but be the first city to scare off an intruder and/or put the fear of God into the people who want to do harm to the way we like to live in the USA as a young nation that is learning to get it together?

If one city can be referred to as the city of brotherly love, then can we be known as a city of motherly love?

You can now weigh the pros and cons to give you and others a greater opportunity to create profits on all levels of growth, tangible and intangible. Are you going to cut yourself in or cut yourself out? To cut yourself in, contact the author.

There is one problem that lots of people have. They want you to join in with them in their illnesses. They want you to be of a richness that is free of an illness like theirs in order for them to enjoy themselves in their ill, ill-will.

The Rules are Simple to Follow

We are not just dropping bread crumbs to have someone or something follow the trail to a trap. We are leading people with a revelation that they help to make come true. We are also teaching them how to trap Satan by not letting him trap them.

The consequences are plain as day. The walk to a kind of unified victory is to not just be won for those who may have it all, but for those with little or almost none who are unable to get in where they fit in. Because of their lack, it takes people like us to unstack the odds against them.

The picture of the repercussion of love that will come from this, will be felt all over the places that it is released in to let the world know that the Lord is still in charge. Whoever believes in him will have everlasting life.

So call this what you want, it could become a play that Shakespeare has inspired of a mystery of a Sherlock Holmes. Don't think it is some kind of jive. The levels that take you from one book to another may actually be like a lock that a ship has to go through that has to go step by step like the Panama Canal. Therefore, this can become a trip around the world with no luggage.

Replace the word world with universe the one that is on the inside of you. Top it off with one fact, you know you as I do better than I do, but the Lord knows us better. That is why we can trust him and love one another. If his plan has a way to clear a pathway to see a brighter frontier because it takes us on a frontier when we go inside of ourselves to learn to do his will. When we come out it is a plan of the future to follow.

Therefore, will you take the frontier walk or trip to not only increase in the body of Christ but to help to perform the miracles the Lord has put in charge on some people's heart to do, as I have been charged.

Dr. Tracy E. Bush, doctor of the process of learning to teach the Lord's revelations to come true. The kind of doctor I am speaking on that I have been called by some is a doctor of peace. I like to think of myself as a peacemaker.

I have even heard a man once say he had to one day tell a storm not to come upon his home because if it had it would have torn it down. I consider him a man that is a doctor of peace but I don't believe I have the same kind of gift as he had. I believe he can control the power of a tornado. I think I have the power to move away an atmospheric storm. Well different gifts for different people. Thank God for any kind we may be blessed with.

Matthew 5:9
9. Blessed are the peacemakers, for they shall be called sons of God.

Note: I like to think when the bugs called Cicadas are gone away the rest of any kind of negativity will be also gone in Cleveland, Ohio believing this. It doesn't hurt a thing. Can we call this a human interest story also of a man who wants an old bridge he used to cross as a child to come back to life for others to experience?

We are in need of money to get this information out. There is a GoFundMe account available, gofundme.com/nzp42cys, to receive donations. Your donations will also help fund a spiritual learning center to help young adults and teens as a free service in the inner City of Cleveland.

Thank you for your attention to this matter. For more information regarding Bro. Bush or books he has written, email tb.bthpm@gmail.com or visit www.boundtoheaven.org. To help get the books that you may need, it can help to also pay for promotions.

Thank you,
Bro. Tracy E. Bush
A Messenger in the Body of Christ

Philippians 4:17
Not that I seek the gift, but I seek the fruit that abounds to your account

Acts 20:24
But none of these things move me; nor do I count my life dear to myself, so that I may finish my race with joy, and the ministry which I received from the Lord Jesus, to testify to the gospel of the grace of God.

Notes

_____

_____

_____

_____

_____

_____

_____

_____

_____

_____

_____

_____

_____

_____

_____